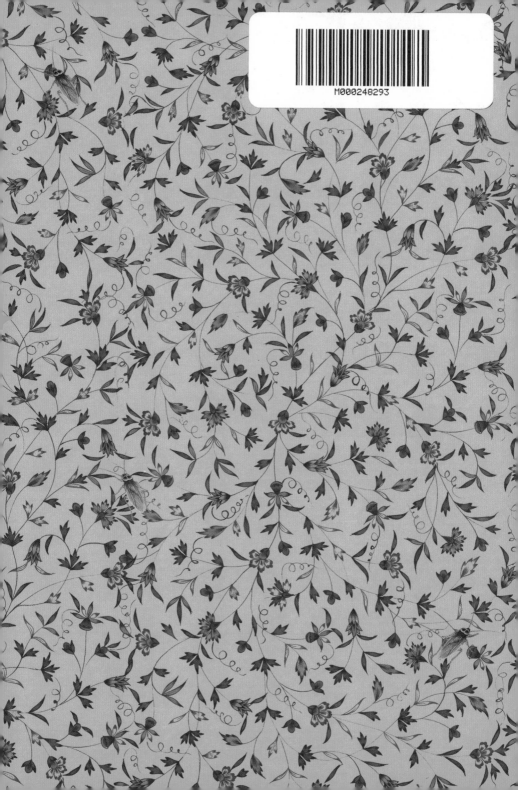

M000248293

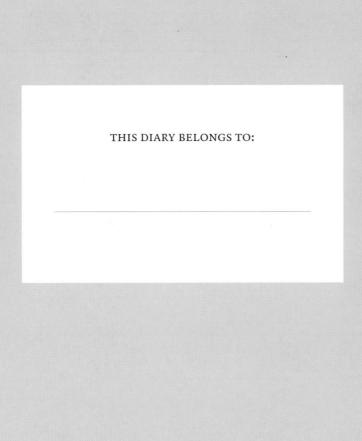

THIS DIARY BELONGS TO:

_____

London Review of Books
28 Little Russell Street, London WC1A 2HN

ISBN 978-1-800819-23-8

Typeset by LRB (London) Ltd

The text is set in Quadraat Pro

Compiled by: Sam Kinchin-Smith
Edited by: Jean McNicol
Design: Lola Bunting, Christopher G. Thompson
Artwork: Alexander Gorlizki

Printed and bound in Turkey by Imago

Distributed to bookshops by
Profile Books Ltd, 29 Cloth Fair, London EC1A 7JQ

lrb.co.uk

LRB DIARY FOR 2024

15 October 1914. Leafed through the diary a little. Had a sort of inkling of the organisation of such a life.

Editorial Note

'There are many perils in writing about Kafka,' according to Alan Bennett. 'His work has been garrisoned by armies of critics, with some fifteen thousand books about him at the last count. As there is a Fortress Freud so is there a Fortress Kafka, Kafka his own castle. For admission a certain high seriousness must be deemed essential, and I am not sure I have it.' The archive of the *London Review of Books* allows us to trace the treatment of some particularly popular subjects over more than forty years. Fortress Freud looms large, as do the garrisons of Thatcher, Shakespeare and Hitler, but Kafka's castle has one of the largest armies of critics. That's why he is the focus of our Diary for 2024, the centenary of his death.

We've added quotations from Kafka's own diaries to the weekly planner pages for additional inspiration/nihilism. These are taken from Ross Benjamin's new translation, published by Schocken Books, which retains Kafka's eccentricities of punctuation and grammar. Many of the extracts from LRB pieces have been edited for clarity. A list of links to the originals can be found at lrb.me/kafka

2024

JANUARY

M	T	W	T	F	S	S
1	2	3	4	5	6	7
8	9	10	11	12	13	14
15	16	17	18	19	20	21
22	23	24	25	26	27	28
29	30	31	1	2	3	4
5	6	7	8	9	10	11

FEBRUARY

M	T	W	T	F	S	S
29	30	31	1	2	3	4
5	6	7	8	9	10	11
12	13	14	15	16	17	18
19	20	21	22	23	24	25
26	27	28	29	1	2	3
4	5	6	7	8	9	10

MARCH

M	T	W	T	F	S	S
26	27	28	29	1	2	3
4	5	6	7	8	9	10
11	12	13	14	15	16	17
18	19	20	21	22	23	24
25	26	27	28	29	30	31
1	2	3	4	5	6	7

APRIL

M	T	W	T	F	S	S
1	2	3	4	5	6	7
8	9	10	11	12	13	14
15	16	17	18	19	20	21
22	23	24	25	26	27	28
29	30	1	2	3	4	5
6	7	8	9	10	11	12

MAY

M	T	W	T	F	S	S
29	30	1	2	3	4	5
6	7	8	9	10	11	12
13	14	15	16	17	18	19
20	21	22	23	24	25	26
27	28	29	30	31	1	2
3	4	5	6	7	8	9

JUNE

M	T	W	T	F	S	S
27	28	29	30	31	1	2
3	4	5	6	7	8	9
10	11	12	13	14	15	16
17	18	19	20	21	22	23
24	25	26	27	28	29	30
1	2	3	4	5	6	7

JULY

M	T	W	T	F	S	S
1	2	3	4	5	6	7
8	9	10	11	12	13	14
15	16	17	18	19	20	21
22	23	24	25	26	27	28
29	30	31	1	2	3	4
5	6	7	8	9	10	11

AUGUST

M	T	W	T	F	S	S
29	30	31	1	2	3	4
5	6	7	8	9	10	11
12	13	14	15	16	17	18
19	20	21	22	23	24	25
26	27	28	29	30	31	1
2	3	4	5	6	7	8

SEPTEMBER

M	T	W	T	F	S	S
26	27	28	29	30	31	1
2	3	4	5	6	7	8
9	10	11	12	13	14	15
16	17	18	19	20	21	22
23	24	25	26	27	28	29
30	1	2	3	4	5	6

OCTOBER

M	T	W	T	F	S	S
30	1	2	3	4	5	6
7	8	9	10	11	12	13
14	15	16	17	18	19	20
21	22	23	24	25	26	27
28	29	30	31	1	2	3
4	5	6	7	8	9	10

NOVEMBER

M	T	W	T	F	S	S
28	29	30	31	1	2	3
4	5	6	7	8	9	10
11	12	13	14	15	16	17
18	19	20	21	22	23	24
25	26	27	28	29	30	1
2	3	4	5	6	7	8

DECEMBER

M	T	W	T	F	S	S
25	26	27	28	29	30	1
2	3	4	5	6	7	8
9	10	11	12	13	14	15
16	17	18	19	20	21	22
23	24	25	26	27	28	29
30	31	1	2	3	4	5

JANUARY

M	T	W	T	F	S	S
30	31	1	2	3	4	5
6	7	8	9	10	11	12
13	14	15	16	17	18	19
20	21	22	23	24	25	26
27	28	29	30	31	1	2
3	4	5	6	7	8	9

FEBRUARY

M	T	W	T	F	S	S
27	28	29	30	31	1	2
3	4	5	6	7	8	9
10	11	12	13	14	15	16
17	18	19	20	21	22	23
24	25	26	27	28	1	2
3	4	5	6	7	8	9

MARCH

M	T	W	T	F	S	S
24	25	26	27	28	1	2
3	4	5	6	7	8	9
10	11	12	13	14	15	16
17	18	19	20	21	22	23
24	25	26	27	28	29	30
31	1	2	3	4	5	6

APRIL

M	T	W	T	F	S	S
31	1	2	3	4	5	6
7	8	9	10	11	12	13
14	15	16	17	18	19	20
21	22	23	24	25	26	27
28	29	30	1	2	3	4
5	6	7	8	9	10	11

MAY

M	T	W	T	F	S	S
28	29	30	1	2	3	4
5	6	7	8	9	10	11
12	13	14	15	16	17	18
19	20	21	22	23	24	25
26	27	28	29	30	31	1
2	3	4	5	6	7	8

JUNE

M	T	W	T	F	S	S
26	27	28	29	30	31	1
2	3	4	5	6	7	8
9	10	11	12	13	14	15
16	17	18	19	20	21	22
23	24	25	26	27	28	29
30	1	2	3	4	5	6

JULY

M	T	W	T	F	S	S
30	1	2	3	4	5	6
7	8	9	10	11	12	13
14	15	16	17	18	19	20
21	22	23	24	25	26	27
28	29	30	31	1	2	3
4	5	6	7	8	9	10

AUGUST

M	T	W	T	F	S	S
28	29	30	31	1	2	3
4	5	6	7	8	9	10
11	12	13	14	15	16	17
18	19	20	21	22	23	24
25	26	27	28	29	30	31
1	2	3	4	5	6	7

SEPTEMBER

M	T	W	T	F	S	S
1	2	3	4	5	6	7
8	9	10	11	12	13	14
15	16	17	18	19	20	21
22	23	24	25	26	27	28
29	30	1	2	3	4	5
6	7	8	9	10	11	12

OCTOBER

M	T	W	T	F	S	S
29	30	1	2	3	4	5
6	7	8	9	10	11	12
13	14	15	16	17	18	19
20	21	22	23	24	25	26
27	28	29	30	31	1	2
3	4	5	6	7	8	9

NOVEMBER

M	T	W	T	F	S	S
27	28	29	30	31	1	2
3	4	5	6	7	8	9
10	11	12	13	14	15	16
17	18	19	20	21	22	23
24	25	26	27	28	29	30
1	2	3	4	5	6	7

DECEMBER

M	T	W	T	F	S	S
1	2	3	4	5	6	7
8	9	10	11	12	13	14
15	16	17	18	19	20	21
22	23	24	25	26	27	28
29	30	31	1	2	3	4
5	6	7	8	9	10	11

Patricia Lockwood
on Kafka and Covid-19

Kafka had consumption, which everyone else also had at that
time: look at them up on the tops of mountains, men coughing
spots in love with women coughing spots, so that you could
draw lines between them until the whole world was filled in.
It was a comfort to read him in a year when everyone again had
the same disease. More specifically her, for in that moment she
was everyone. She thought she could work through him, if she
could not work through herself; she thought she could use his
hands, if she could not use her own.

Vol. 44 No. 6 · 24 March 2022

1 Monday   NEW YEAR'S DAY

2 Tuesday   2ND JANUARY (SCOT)

3 Wednesday

4 Thursday

'Glaube und Heimat' by Schönherr. The wet fingers of the gallery patrons below me, who wipe their eyes. (1911)

5 Friday

6 Saturday   7 Sunday

Alan Bennett
on Kafka in utero

It seems pretty well accepted now that much of one's life, including the length of it and the weaknesses to which one will be prone, is decided in the womb. This would please Kafka, or at any rate confirm his worst fears: to be sentenced to death before one is even born would be for him a kind of apotheosis.

Vol. 16 No. 20 · 20 October 1994

8 Monday

9 Tuesday

10 Wednesday

11 Thursday

12 Friday

There are possibilities for me, certainly, but under what stone do they lie? (1914)

13 Saturday   14 Sunday

Rivka Galchen
on Kafka's attention-seeking

Young Kafka was perennially convinced he was about to fail out of school, despite always getting top marks and the approval of his teachers. Even stranger, the older Kafka held onto these feelings. In a letter to his father, he wrote:

> Often in my mind's eye I saw the frightful assembly of the teachers (the Gymnasium is only the most obvious example, but it was similar all around me), with them meeting, when I had passed the first class, and then in the second class, when I had passed that, and then in the third, and so on, in order to examine this unique, outrageous case, to discover how I, the most incapable, or at least the most ignorant of all, had succeeded in creeping up as far as this class, which now, when everybody's attention had at last been focused on me, would of course instantly spew me out, to the jubilation of all the righteous liberated from this nightmare.

In other words, he needed more attention. And in a rare finale to the child epic – when will I be the centre of tremendous attention? – his nightmare comes true, with the last ambivalent twist of the attention being worship.

Vol. 39 No. 6 · 16 March 2017

15 Monday

16 Tuesday

17 Wednesday

Some deny the misery by pointing to the sun, he denies the sun by pointing to the misery. (1920)

18 Thursday

19 Friday

20 Saturday   21 Sunday

Adam Phillips
on Kafka and swimming

Two months after writing about the Olympic champion, Kafka, who was himself a keen swimmer, wrote something else about swimming: 'I can swim like the others, only I have a better memory than the others, I have not forgotten my former not-being-able-to-swim. But because I have not forgotten it, the being-able-to-swim does me no good, and I still cannot swim.' Since there was – and still is – a time before we could swim we are always, somewhere in ourselves, people who can't swim. In this story, exclusion always precedes inclusion, and we are always haunted by our being left out. The person who can't swim is always with us. And the question, as Freud attempted to formulate and formalise, is this: what kind of relationship do we have with these former selves? As children growing up, we are initiated in sociability and eventually included in the adult world – or at least that's the official story. But the fact that we were once unable to swim means we still can't really swim, even if we win an Olympic swimming medal.

Vol. 43 No. 10 · 20 May 2021

22 Monday

23 Tuesday

24 Wednesday

25 Thursday

To say that you abandoned me would be very unjust, but that I was abandoned, and at times horribly, is true. (1922)

26 Friday

27 Saturday   28 Sunday

Anne Hollander
on Kafka and his body

It appears that Kafka was personally interested in the body-culture systems that flourished in German society at the time, and that he followed for years the gymnastics manual of one J.P. Müller, which had a picture of the *Apoxyomenos* on the cover and photos of the author inside, a mustachioed version solemnly demonstrating the prescribed movements in the nude. Kafka was also interested in the eurythmics of Dalcroze, and visited his school; and he was interested in the dress reform movement, on which he attended lectures. But gymnastics and acrobatics especially fascinated Kafka, who felt himself to be too tall, too thin, too awkward and physically fragmented. His early devotion to sartorial elegance was among other things an attempt to harmonise himself, an effort continued by his body-building regime. His health did give way to tuberculosis, despite all the Müller exercises, the vegetarian diet, the abstinence from alcohol, the many hikes in the country. But the bodily effort had not been made to cheat physical death. Linked to the well-cut suits and to similar efforts in his writing, it was a bid for aesthetic immortality; and that he achieved.

Vol. 14 No. 18 · 24 September 1992

29 Monday

30 Tuesday

31 Wednesday

1 Thursday

2 Friday

The door opened a crack. A revolver appeared and an outstretched arm. (1914)

3 Saturday   4 Sunday

Gabriel Josipovici
on Kafka's mysteriousness

There was something about the man which transcended the works, a quality glimpsed through the works which could neither be pinned down nor reduced to a simple (or complex) issue about interpretation. At the time, it seemed difficult to bring this quality into focus. Was our curiosity about Kafka any different from our curiosity about Joyce or Scott Fitzgerald? It was, but how and why? Answers to these questions began to emerge as more and more of his writings began to appear: his diaries, his letter to his father, the batch of letters to Milena Jesenská and, finally, the enormous volume of letters to Felice Bauer, the woman he was twice engaged to and who, with his father, was surely the central external factor in his life. Of the twelve volumes of Kafka's writings in the German edition, just over half are devoted to what might be called 'non-fiction'. But the strange thing about these letters and diaries was not that they made us realise how much more autobiographical the novels were than we had thought, but that they forced us to revise our notions of where the boundaries might lie between fiction and non-fiction. They did not so much open Kafka up to us as give us a great many more examples of his perennial mysteriousness.

Vol. 3 No. 4 · 5 March 1981

5 Monday

6 Tuesday

7 Wednesday

Complete standstill. Endless torments. (1915)

8 Thursday

9 Friday

10 Saturday   11 Sunday

Christian Lorentzen
imagines his Kafka book

I put my fork in a tomato and then it came to me. I jotted down the book proposal on a napkin. Provisional title: *My Friend Franz: Chronicle of a Life Not a Little Kafkaesque.*

Chapter 1: Age 13. Read *Metamorphosis* – own body undergoing changes never anticipated. Develop a passionate interest in entomology. Crippling phobia about apples.

Chapter 2: At university I read *The Trial*. Lifelong persecution complex begins.

Chapter 3: Close reading of 'The Penal Colony'. New Year's Eve in Prague, 2000. Wake with BE JUST tattoo on right shoulder blade.

Chapter 4: I move to the city. Series of loathsome day jobs while writing book reviews late at night, exactly the time Kafka would compose his short stories. Echoing a letter he wrote to prospective father-in-law Carl Bauer, I send a text message to a girlfriend, cancelling dinner: 'I have no aptitude for going out to restaurants. All I am is book reviewing and want to be nothing else. Everything that is not book reviewing bores me. Sorry, babe.'

12 Monday

13 Tuesday

14 Wednesday

15 Thursday

16 Friday

17 Saturday   18 Sunday

Alan Bennett
on the Parents of Art

Hermann Kafka has had such a consistently bad press that it's hard not to feel a sneaking sympathy for him, as for all the Parents of Art. They never get it right. They bring up a child badly and he turns out a writer, posterity never forgives them – though without that unfortunate upbringing the writer might never have written a word. They bring up a child well and he never does write a word. Do it right and posterity never hears about the parents: do it wrong and posterity never hears about anything else.

They fuck you up your Mum and Dad, and if you're planning on writing that's probably a good thing. But if you are planning on writing and they haven't fucked you up, well, you've got nothing to go on, so then they've fucked you up good and proper.

Kafka may have been frightened that he was more like his father than he cared to admit. In a letter to Felice Bauer he indulges in the fantasy of being a large piece of wood, pressed against the body of a cook 'who is holding the knife along the side of this stiff log (somewhere in the region of my hip) slicing off shavings to light the fire'. Many conclusions could be drawn from this image, some glibber than others. One of them is that Kafka would have liked to have been a chip off the old block.

19 Monday

20 Tuesday

Imperceptible life. Perceptible failure. (1922)

21 Wednesday

A walk through the streets in the evening. The back and forth of the women. (1922)

22 Thursday

In the streets. A thought. (1922)

23 Friday

24 Saturday   25 Sunday

Frederick Seidel
from 'Worst When It's Poetry'

Here's a naked fellow dressed up in some clothes,
Arrogantly flaunting what he actually loathes –
The Savile Row swagger and the nonchalant pose!
He's who he isn't and he makes sure it shows.

I'm Nobody! Who are you?
I'm thinking, what would mother do?
And what would Kafka if he knew?
Emily Dickinson was Nobody, too!

I'd say the day looks like there's nothing new.
It's simply someone the sky is talking to.
Sprinklers on Central Park's Great Lawn are hissing mist,
A smell simply too delicious to exist.

Sweet, sweet, sweet! You drown in it, I've drowned.
The currents undersea wave our hearts around.
You'll be so happy that I'm cured of snoring and now I snore
No more.

26 Monday

Better self-confidence. Heartbeat closer to my wishes. The hiss of the gas light over me. (1912)

27 Tuesday

I have no time to write letters twice. (1912)

28 Wednesday

29 Thursday

1 Friday

2 Saturday   3 Sunday

Rivka Galchen
on reading (about) Kafka

We might ask ourselves why we would read a biography of Kafka when we could instead just read Kafka. Why make breakfast, when you can just read Kafka? Why watch television or trim your fingernails when you could just read Kafka?

Vol. 36 No. 23 · 4 December 2014

4 Monday

5 Tuesday

6 Wednesday

7 Thursday

8 Friday

Was reproached the day before yesterday because of the factory. Then for an hour on the sofa thought about jumping-out-the-window. (1912)

9 Saturday   10 Sunday

Michael Wood
on the Kafkaesque

I began to wonder whether the Kafkaesque is not, as the OED tautologically says, the name of a 'state of affairs or a state of mind described by Kafka', but rather a form of strangeness that is more ordinary than we think. We call it strange because we want it to be strange. Kafka didn't simply describe it, and he didn't invent it. He blew its cover, and more important still, revealed its alarming frequency. It's not for nothing that one of his weirdest, most wonderful stories is called 'A Common Confusion', literally 'an everyday confusion'.

Vol. 30 No. 22 · 20 November 2008

11 Monday

Yesterday unbearable. Why doesn't everyone take part in the evening meal. It would just be so nice. (1912)

12 Tuesday

13 Wednesday

14 Thursday

15 Friday

16 Saturday

17 Sunday

Colm Tóibín
on Kafka and gay literature

The gay past contains silence and fear as well as Whitman's poems and Shakespeare's sonnets, and this may be why the work of Kafka continues to interest gay readers so much, and why it is so easy to find a gay subtext in Kafka's novels and stories. Some critics go further, however. 'It is only when one reads the totality of Kafka's writings,' Ruth Tiefenbrun has written,

> that it becomes apparent that the predicament of all his heroes is based on the fact that they are all homosexuals . . . Since Kafka spent his entire lifetime deliberately concealing his homosexuality, it is not at all surprising that there are relatively few overt references . . . Kafka shares with his fellow deviants their most distinctive trait: their simultaneous need to conceal and to exhibit themselves.

Gregory Woods in *A History of Gay Literature* considers Ruth Tiefenbrun's theories too reductive of Kafka's genius, but convincing in relation to his work. 'The question we have to ask ourselves,' he writes, 'is whether, in order to appreciate the texts in question as gay literature, we have to accept a largely speculative narrative about the author's life . . . In short, why should a text not be its own proof of the readings one performs upon it?' The argument then moves from what Kafka meant, to what Kafka really meant, to what we mean when we read Kafka. I think we mean a great deal.

18 Monday   ST PATRICK'S DAY (SUBSTITUTE DAY)

19 Tuesday

20 Wednesday

21 Thursday

22 Friday

23 Saturday   24 Sunday

Patricia Lockwood
on Kafka and pornography

Why was Kafka possible to read, when everything else looked like the alphabet ejaculated at random on the ground? Kafka ejaculated the alphabet in order. Every so often an article came out in the *New Yorker* about how he masturbated constantly to the craziest porn – she couldn't remember exactly what, but maybe etchings, and pictures of bloomers, and puppets freaking out on their strings – so that it was a wonder he had any time left to write. Or: 'Clothes brushed against me, once I seized a ribbon that ornamented the back of a girl's skirt and let her draw it out of my hand as I walked away . . .' Maybe the porn was like that.

Vol. 44 No. 6 · 24 March 2022

25 Monday

The broom sweeping the rug in the next room sounds like the jerkily moving train of a dress. (1912)

26 Tuesday

Just don't overestimate what I've written, in that way I make what is to be written unattainable. (1912)

27 Wednesday

28 Thursday

29 Friday   GOOD FRIDAY

The pleasure in the bathroom. – Gradual recognition. The afternoons I spent with my hair. (1912)

30 Saturday   31 Sunday

Elif Batuman
on Kafka's insect

As Nabokov himself once established with entomological diagrams, Kafka had no clear picture of what his insect looked like. On the other hand, he probably had a clear picture of the framed magazine picture on Gregor's wall ('a lady fitted out with a fur hat and fur boa who sat upright, raising a heavy fur muff that covered the whole of her lower arm towards the viewer') and the 'cool, leather sofa' and the cigarettes and the textile samples. No matter how you showed the insect, it would be a lie. But physical things, the mass-produced brothers and sisters, have a certain truth. Like Orthodox icons, they are 'images not made by hands': symbols that are also somehow identical to the things they represent. When you watch a film adaptation of a novel, you always have to stop and ask yourself what are the odds that Eugene Onegin happened to look exactly like Ralph Fiennes, and yet a teapot from the right historical period is a real part of the world that created the character and plot. If you had enough of the textile samples and magazine pictures and sofas, maybe you could re-create the insect.

Vol. 34 No. 11 · 7 June 2012

1 Monday EASTER MONDAY (NOT SCOT)

2 Tuesday

3 Wednesday

4 Thursday

5 Friday

6 Saturday 7 Sunday

Amit Chaudhuri
on Kafka's social satire

A feature of Kafka's writing is its extraordinary social and cultural pitch; its exploration, not just of existential man alone in the universe, but of the life of the middle-class individual, and, especially in The Trial, of the European bourgeoisie in the early 20th century, with its crushing, illogically simultaneous emphasis on material success and old-world dignity and culture. In Metamorphosis, Kafka uses music to define class and social position: Gregor's sister's violin-playing betokens the family's desperate pretensions, with the violin a means of distinguishing oneself both from the desolation of the working class and the vulgarity of the nouveau riche. The lodgers' growing boredom as they listen, and the image of Gregor, turned into an insect, hidden behind the door, the only one truly engrossed in the music, evoke, among other things, a profound nostalgia for one's absolutely ordinary, but, to oneself, irreplaceable position in society. Food, too, is part of Kafka's social exploration, and, in his list of what is appealing to Gregor's appetite, Kafka gives us a parody of food as a social code. The list is both playful and painfully attentive, reminding us once more that the real 'metamorphosis' in the story is the transformation of the stable and precious symbols of a middle-class world into something else. It is not that Kafka's allegories represent the social: they are in complex ways informed and transformed by the social.

Vol. 17 No. 11 · 8 June 1995

8 Monday

9 Tuesday

10 Wednesday

Eternal youth is impossible; even if there were no other hindrance, self-observation would make it impossible. (1922)

11 Thursday

12 Friday

13 Saturday   14 Sunday

Joe Dunthorne
on Kafka's favourite book

Heinrich von Kleist's most striking quality is his narrative speed. His fiction often reads like synopsis, each sentence burning through scenes to which other writers would dedicate a whole chapter. Nowhere is this better displayed than in his novella *Michael Kohlhaas*, first published in its entirety in 1810. It tells the story of a husband, father, horse dealer and 'good citizen' who, while attempting to cross into Saxony to sell his wares, gets ripped off and mocked by the Junker of the castle at the border. Kohlhaas responds to this indignity with such fervour that, just 36 pages later, he has sacrificed his home; seen his wife killed in the act of trying to help him; looted and torched the offending castle; and, with a small army of men, chased the Junker first to Wittenberg, a town they swiftly burn to the ground, then on to Leipzig, where Kohlhaas is proclaimed the leader of a new 'provisional world government' whose sole purpose is to 'punish with fire and sword all those who took the side of the Junker'. What makes this breakneck escalation so remarkable is that it feels believable – even reasonable. We are firmly on the side of the madman.

It's not surprising that Kafka loved this book. He read it ten times. 'It carries me along on waves of wonder,' he wrote, which is a very Kafka response to a story in which everyone suffers terribly and/or dies.

Vol. 43 No. 7 · 1 April 2021

15 Monday

16 Tuesday

17 Wednesday

18 Thursday

19 Friday

I will have 3 weeks to myself. Is that called being treated cruelly? (1916)

20 Saturday   21 Sunday

Michael Wood
on Kafka the bureaucrat

'The crows maintain that a single crow could destroy heaven. This is beyond doubt, but doesn't prove anything against heaven, since heaven means, precisely, the impossibility of crows.' 'To believe in progress is not to believe that progress has already happened. That would not be a belief.' 'There can be a knowledge of the devilish, but no belief in it, because there is nothing more devilish than what already exists.' 'If it had been possible to build the Tower of Babel without climbing it, it would have been allowed.' 'In the battle between yourself and the world, support the world.' 'Goodness is in a certain sense comfortless.' The writer here is not the victim but the merciless and stylish analyst; not the land surveyor but the surveyor of the arrangement. In this sense it is surely a mistake, as Stanley Corngold suggests it is, to pit Kafka's bureaucracy against its 'hapless supplicant'. He is bureaucrat and supplicant, perhaps more bureaucrat than supplicant. What saves him from the Devil's service, redeems him at the last minute, as if he were Goethe's Faust swept up by the angels, is neither the system nor a fight against the system but his sheer lucidity about the system's fragile supremacy.

22 Monday

23 Tuesday

24 Wednesday

25 Thursday

26 Friday

27 Saturday   28 Sunday

Anne Carson
from 'A Fragment of Ibykos Translated Six Ways'

[Ibykos fr. 286 as pp. 136-37 of *Conversations with Kafka* by Gustav Janouch]

In the end, on the one hand, all those who sit behind us at the
cash desks,
being engaged in the most destructive and hopeless rebellion
there could
ever be,
where everything human [has been betrayed]
and
beneath the burden of existence
stock phrases,
with a gentle indefinable smile,
arouse suspicion.

29 Monday

30 Tuesday

1 Wednesday

2 Thursday

3 Friday

4 Saturday   5 Sunday

Alan Bennett
on misremembering *The Trial*

The readers or non-readers of *The Trial* remember it wrong. Its reputation is as a tale about man and bureaucracy, a fable appropriate to the office block. One recalls the office in Orson Welles's film – a vast hangar in which hundreds of clerks foil at identical desks to an identical routine. In fact, *The Trial* is set in small rooms in dark houses in surroundings that are pictur- esque, romantic and downright quaint. For the setting of *The Trial* there is no blaming the planners. It is all on an impeccably human scale.

The topography that oppressed Kafka does not oppress us. Kafka's fearful universe is constructed out of burrows and garrets and cubbyholes on back staircases. It is nearer to Dickens and Alice and even to the cosiness of *The Wind in the Willows* than it is to our own particular emptinesses. Our shorthand for desol- ation is quite different: the assembly line, the fence festoon- ed with polythene rags, the dead land between the legs of the motorway. But it is ours. It isn't Kafka's. Or, to put it another way, the trouble with Kafka is that he didn't know the word 'Kafkaesque'. However, those who see *The Trial* as a trailer for totalitarian bureaucracy might be confirmed in this view on finding that the premises in Dzherzhinsky Square in Moscow now occupied by the Lubyanka Prison formerly housed another institution, the Rossiya Insurance Company.

Vol. 9 No. 14 · 23 July 1987

6 Monday

My parents seem to have found a nice apartment for F. and me, I spent a nice afternoon wandering around uselessly. Will they lay me in my grave too after a life made happy by their care? (1914)

7 Tuesday

8 Wednesday

9 Thursday

10 Friday

11 Saturday   12 Sunday

Hans Keller
on Kafka at the football

Reportage about any activity that involves expert knowledge needs two professionalisms, not one – not only the activity's own expertise, that is to say, but also reporting expertise, which, in principle, is a scientific quality, as regards both the expert's power of observation and his sheer conscience about getting things right. A great writer will ineluctably evince such a scientific aptitude, his imagination quite apart: Max Brod recounts that he was staggered at Franz Kafka's detailed report on a football match they had seen together; Kafka had suggested that they should try and see who could remember more, minute details included. No wonder mass communication is a grave problem – amazing, though, that the fact is not universally realised.

Vol. 4 No. 14 · 5 August 1982

13 Monday

14 Tuesday

15 Wednesday

16 Thursday

17 Friday

18 Saturday   19 Sunday

Dan Jacobson
on Kafka, Kierkegaard and Nietzsche

Though Kafka is one of the major figures of literary modernism, we can perhaps gain a better understanding of his work by looking back rather than forward, and by trying to see it in relation to two great 19th-century masters of paradox and self-contradiction, Nietzsche and Kierkegaard. Nietzsche was preoccupied with the transformation (in individuals, classes and races) of weakness into strength, and with the modes in which or through which strength could be prevailed on to submit to weakness; Kierkegaard proclaimed dread and faith, the absurd and the absolute, to be wedded indissolubly together. However, each of these men saw himself ultimately as a servant of the 'positive' element – strength in Nietzsche's case, faith in Kierkegaard's – of the conjunction which he put at the centre of his work. Kafka, by contrast, takes no sides in his fiction: or rather, by expressing them both with an extraordinary purity and intensity, he reveals that for him the two sides – strength and weakness, the absolute and the absurd – are one.

Vol. 3 No. 22 · 3 December 1981

20 Monday

21 Tuesday

22 Wednesday

23 Thursday

24 Friday

25 Saturday   26 Sunday

Adam Phillips
on giving up

'From a certain point there is no more turning back. That is
the point that must be reached.' This is one of Kafka's Zürau
Aphorisms, written during the war – between 1917 and 1918 –
just after he received a diagnosis of the tuberculosis that would
eventually kill him. 'From a certain point there is no more turning back. That is the point that must be reached.' Why? Because
there is always the temptation to give up? Or, more suggestively,
because there is always the temptation to turn back, to turn
round: to go back, say, to the past, to the place from which one
started, to retrace your steps; or simply to turn back to the time
when you can choose to give up, or choose again what you really
want to do; as though progress, or completion or commitment,
depends on reaching the point from which there is no more
turning back. At that point, it is implied, we have finally made
our decision. The crisis of choice is over; we are no longer in
search of exits and alibis; we are no longer seduced by alter-
natives and deferrals. It is the point at which we know what we
want; we are no longer the complicated, conflicted creatures we
were until this point. Our doubts are finally in abeyance. We are,
in a certain sense, free. The point from which there is no more
turning back suggests, of course, that there has already been a
certain amount of turning back, or a certain amount of wanting
to turn back. As though a desire to turn back is what we always
have to contend with – as a temptation, or simply as a choice.

27 Monday

Much unhappiness since the last entry. Am going to ruin. To go so senselessly and unnecessarily to ruin. (1915)

28 Tuesday

29 Wednesday

30 Thursday

31 Friday

1 Saturday   2 Sunday

Jenny Turner
on Kafka and *The Lord of the Rings*

Frodo's sufferings are wonderfully evocative of the self-pity and self-mythologisation that tend to come with depression. One always does feel that life is a struggle between the forces of good and the forces of evil. (Guess which side poor little me is on?) One always does feel oneself to be labouring like an insect across a blasted plain. One always does remember the great wrongs done to one, and feel so hurt by them that one will never heal. How much more gratifying to feel one has been wounded by a Morgul-knife instead of merely stabbed in the back by someone nasty. How much more satisfactory to think one has been defeated, not by ordinary slings and arrows, but in one's heroic struggle to save the world. 'I tried to save the Shire, and it has been saved, but not for me': these are Frodo's words, just before he sails away into oblivion. It's the 'hope, but not for us' of Kafka. The real War of the Ring has nothing to do with how many trolls and orcs Mordor can muster. It's a struggle with despair.

3 Monday

4 Tuesday

5 Wednesday

The inner advantages that mediocre literary works draw from the fact that their authors are still alive and pursuing them. The actual sense of growing obsolete. (1913)

6 Thursday

7 Friday

8 Saturday   9 Sunday

Penelope Fitzgerald
on Rebecca West on Kafka

With her limitless energy and enthusiasm, Rebecca West called
for harmony, but not for moderation. All that the reader can do,
very often, is to trust the driver as her arguments bowl along in
splendid sentences or collect themselves for a pause. 'Men and
women see totally different aspects of reality.' 'A great deal of
what Kafka wrote is not worth studying.' 'Authentic art never
has an explicit religious and moral content.' These are sweeping
statements – though sweeping, of course, can be a worthwhile
activity.

Vol. 9 No. 20 · 12 November 1987

10 Monday

11 Tuesday

12 Wednesday

13 Thursday

14 Friday

15 Saturday

16 Sunday

Aharon Appelfeld
on Kafka's different registers

To my surprise he spoke to me not only in my mother tongue, but also in another language which I knew intimately, the language of the absurd. I knew what he was talking about. It wasn't a secret language for me and I didn't need any explications. I had come from the camps and the forests, from a world that embodied the absurd, and nothing in that world was foreign to me. What was surprising was this: how could a man who had never been there know so much, in precise detail, about that world?

17 Monday

18 Tuesday

19 Wednesday

Slept, woke up, slept, woke up, miserable life. (1910)

20 Thursday

21 Friday

22 Saturday   23 Sunday

Barbara Johnson
on Kafka's love letters

Kafka writes to Felice Bauer: 'Don't deceive yourself, dearest; the cause of the trouble lies not in the distance; on the contrary, it is this very distance that gives me at least the semblance of having some right to you.' He confides to her:

> I have often thought that the best mode of life for me would be to sit in the innermost room of a spacious locked cellar with my writing things and my lamp. Food would be brought and always put down far away from my room . . . For who am I? A shadow who loves you infinitely, but who cannot be drawn into the light.

Vincent Kaufmann comments: 'He needs a presence to vouch for his absence. Letters allow Kafka to show himself for the shadow that he is.' The 'engagement' between Kafka and Bauer is one designed to result not in marriage but in writing.

24 Monday

The parents' grave in which the son ('Pollak, graduate of a commercial academy') is buried too. (1914)

25 Tuesday

26 Wednesday

27 Thursday

28 Friday

29 Saturday   30 Sunday

Rivka Galchen
on Kafka and situation comedy

Often his character recalls both Larry David and Bertie Wooster. Many are the plans that Kafka makes in a manner that ensures their eventual unmaking . . . At times he seems to be living in a situation comedy. When he goes to the countryside to write, he finds it 'extraordinarily beautiful' at first, but by the second day he can't work because he's troubled by a child practising the French horn, by the din from a sawmill and by happy children playing outside, whom he eventually yells at: 'Why don't you go and pick mushrooms?' He then discovers that the children belong to his neighbour, a sleep-deprived shift worker at the local mill who sends his seven children out so that he can get some sleep. At a sanatorium for his TB, Kafka and his friend Klopstock play a practical joke on another resident, a high-ranking Czech officer who conspicuously practises the flute and sketches and paints outdoors. The officer puts on a show of his work; Klopstock and Kafka write up pseudonymous reviews of it, one published in Czech, the other in Hungarian; the mocked officer then comes to Klopstock (in his room with a fever and kept company by Kafka) for a translation of the review. After this successful prank, Kafka sends his sister a spoof article about how Einstein's theory of relativity is pointing the way to a cure for TB; his whole family celebrates the good news, of which he then has to disabuse them.

1 Monday

2 Tuesday

I would never have married a girl with whom I had lived in the same city for a year. (1913)

3 Wednesday

4 Thursday

5 Friday

To have to bear and cause such woes! (1914)

6 Saturday   7 Sunday

Adam Phillips
on being left out

The advantage of lying on the floor, Kafka once noted in his diary, is that there is nowhere else to fall. But this is a freedom from, not a freedom for: he is freed of the anxiety of falling but says nothing about what he wants this freedom to do. Lying on the floor, in other words, is not the precondition for doing something else. If Kafka has a subject, it is exclusion – the feeling of being left out. It is a feeling of being alien, or strange, or unable to participate (or, in his personal life, unable to marry), and he turns this feeling of being excluded into the wish to exclude himself. When Kafka's heroes, or anti-heroes, aren't describing just how excluded they are – even from the Law, which by definition is meant to include everybody – they are discovering in some uncanny way that they have excluded themselves without noticing. And, perhaps worse, without anyone else noticing, or caring.

Vol. 43 No. 10 · 20 May 2021

8 Monday

Began a little. Am a little sleepy. Also forsaken among these complete strangers. (1912)

9 Tuesday

10 Wednesday

11 Thursday

12 Friday   BATTLE OF THE BOYNE (NI)

13 Saturday   **14 Sunday**

Christopher Reid
on Kafka's dreams

Of all writers, perhaps Kafka is the one best equipped to convey the comedy of the ego's misadventures in dreamland: the plainness of his prose and the subtlety of his irony make it hard for the reader to identify just how he achieves his effects. The following diary entry, dated 21 July 1913, shows his mastery:

> Today, in my dream, I invented a new kind of vehicle for a park slope. You take a branch, it needn't be very strong, prop it up on the ground at a slight angle, hold one end in your hand, sit down on it side-saddle, then the whole branch naturally rushes down the slope, since you are sitting on the bough you are carried along at full speed, rocking comfortably on the elastic wood. It is also possible to use the branch to ride up again. The chief advantage, aside from the simplicity of the whole device, lies in the fact that the branch, thin and flexible as it is, can be lowered or raised as necessary and gets through anywhere, even where a person by himself would get through only with difficulty.

That foolish confidence which all dreamers must have felt at some time, especially when learning to fly, the ego's ready 'understanding' of, and acquiescence in, the laws of the dream world, and the ludicrous air of explanatory zeal with which we emerge from our dreams, bearing their marvellous secrets – Kafka has caught these beautifully.

Vol. 5 No. 21 · 17 November 1983

15 Monday

---

16 Tuesday

---

17 Wednesday

---

18 Thursday

---

19 Friday

---

20 Saturday   21 Sunday

Alan Bennett
reads a library book

A sign on Seventh Avenue at Sheridan Square: 'Ears pierced, with or without pain.' I am reading a book on Kafka. It is a library book and someone has marked a passage in the margin with a long, wavering line. I pay the passage special attention without finding it particularly rewarding. As I turn the page the line moves. It is a long, dark hair.

22 Monday

23 Tuesday

Special method of thinking. Emotionally permeated. Everything feels itself to be a thought even in the greatest indefiniteness. (Dostoevsky) (1913)

24 Wednesday

25 Thursday

26 Friday

27 Saturday   28 Sunday

Judith Butler
on Kafka's perfect syntax

His writing effectively opens up the disjunction between clarity – we might even say a certain lucidity and purity of prose – and the horror that is normalised precisely as a consequence of that lucidity. No one can fault the grammar and syntax of Kafka's writing, and no one has ever found emotional excess in his tone; but precisely because of this apparently objective and rigorous mode of writing, a certain horror opens up in the midst of the quotidian, perhaps also an unspeakable grief. Syntax and theme are effectively at war, which means that we might think twice about praising Kafka only for his lucidity. After all, the lucid works as style only insofar as it betrays its own claim to self-sufficiency. Something obscure, if not unspeakable, opens up within the perfect syntax. Indeed, if we consider that recurrent and libellous accusations lurk in the background of his many trials, we can read the narrative voice as a neutralisation of outrage, a linguistic packing away of sorrow that paradoxically brings it to the fore.

29 Monday

30 Tuesday

31 Wednesday

1 Thursday

2 Friday

Germany has declared war on Russia. – Swimming school in the afternoon. (1914)

3 Saturday   4 Sunday

Will Self
on Kafka and the First World War

Prague, already supporting a large refugee population of *Ost-juden* fleeing the 1914 advances of the Russian army into Galicia, was further swamped by wounded and shell-shocked troops returning from the Eastern Front, and a series of defensive battles against the Italians along the Isonzo river. Fuel and food supplies ran low, with each of the city's moieties accusing the other of hoarding. Even the well-to-do Kafkas were subject to privation, and Kafka's mother wrote to Felice Bauer's mother in the New Year that at Yom Kippur 'the fasting came easy, since we've been in training for it all year.' Her etiolated and vegetarian son was always match-fit for privation, but while many commentators have seized on Kafka's journal entry of 5 August 1914 as confirmation of his disengagement from the European Gotterdämmerung – 'I discover in myself nothing but pettiness, indecision, envy and hatred towards those who are fighting, whom I passionately wish all evil' – I am minded to look to the words he wrote in the tiny house in the lee of the Hradčany Castle, and in particular to his description of the wound the eponymous narrator of 'A Country Doctor' finds in 'the right flank' of his young patient, a wound described with a combination of forensic precision and lubricious eroticism: 'at around hip-height, he has a fresh wound as big as my hand. Pink, in many shades, a deep carmine at the centre, lightening towards the periphery, with a soft granular texture, the bleeding at irregular points, and the whole thing as gapingly obvious as a mineshaft.'

From 'Kafka's Wound', a digital essay created by the LRB for the Space in 2012.

5 Monday   AUGUST BANK HOLIDAY (SCOT)

I discover in myself nothing but pettiness, indecision, envy and hatred towards those who are fighting, whom I passionately wish all evil. (1914)

6 Tuesday

7 Wednesday

8 Thursday

And even if everything was unchanged, the spike was still there, crookedly jutting out of his shattered forehead. (1917)

9 Friday

10 Saturday   11 Sunday

Adam Phillips
on Kafka's heroes

Heroes and heroines are people who don't give up; they may
sometimes turn back, but they ultimately persevere. Tragic
heroes are our catastrophic examples of the inability to give
up. In that sense tragedy invites us to re-evaluate certain vers-
ions of giving up. Kafka's heroes are often extremely tenacious:
they very rarely give up, despite the many inducements to do
so (what is heroic in heroism is precisely the resistance to giving up, or perhaps the phobia of giving up). To be arrested for
no apparent reason, to wake up as a beetle: these things would
involve, one might think, at least a strong wish to give up. But
what is striking about Kafka's heroes is how patient they are
in their hopelessness and their helplessness. 'There is hope but
not for us.' Rather tantalisingly, hope does exist; we just can't
have it ourselves. Logically we can then ask: in what sense does
it exist? What relationship can we have with it? We might answer
that it is something we want that eludes us: it exists only in our
wanting it, which may or may not be good grounds for giving up
on it. So to give up on hope would just mean to give up on wanting it, just as giving up is always giving up wanting something or
someone, giving up wanting to be someone. What has always to
be given up, in giving up, is the wanting. 'There is a destination,
but no way there,' Kafka writes in another aphorism. 'What we
refer to as way is hesitation.'

12 Monday

13 Tuesday

14 Wednesday

Coitus as punishment for the happiness of being together. To live as ascetically as possible, more ascetically than a bachelor, that's the only way for me to endure marriage. But her? (1913)

15 Thursday

16 Friday

Nothing either in the office or at home. Wrote a few pages in the Weimar diary. In the evening my poor mother's whimpering because of my not eating. (1912)

17 Saturday   18 Sunday

Anne Hollander
on Kafka and clothes

Gregor, the fearsome beetle, clad in his functional carapace, is the new-made Modern Artist, the ultimate gymnast free to walk on the ceiling and fall without harm, who makes ultimate mockery not only of overstuffed chairs and polite behaviour, of the dress-goods business and of domestic hopes, but of all the old realities – especially artistic ones. This includes the idea at the core of 19th-century novels: that clothes, like facial and bodily traits, always correctly express character. Persons in clean respectable costume are honest and hard-working; persons in showy and flimsy garb are dishonest and morally loose; persons in dirty garments are lazy and unscrupulous, just as persons with sensual lips are sexually susceptible and probably gluttonous, whereas those with tight lips are naturally abstemious.

Horrifying to his family, Gregor's new 'natural body' is beautifully articulated and abstract, like other natural forms and like the frightening emergent forms of modern art, although it is just as far from the costume of Greek nudity, or from reform dress, as it is from ruffles and tight business suits. It shows how form in bodies and clothes, and form in art, can climb free of limiting convention in the modern universe. There, one can see the thing itself, and nothing else. Gregor represents Kafka transformed into writing, as he desired to be. His body, dressed in its perfect animal garment, aspires to the condition of music: but it compromises all life's homely rituals, and it can't comfort him.

19 Monday

20 Tuesday

21 Wednesday

The image of dissatisfaction represented by a street, since everyone is lifting his feet from the place on which he stands to get away. (1912)

22 Thursday

23 Friday

24 Saturday   25 Sunday

David Trotter
on Kafka at the movies

It could be that what we have in the diaries is not a rejection of cinema, but the establishment of a new and idiosyncratic method of viewing. Kafka appears to have viewed film against rather than with the plot. Concentration on a particular scene or effect enabled him to avoid surfeit, to reinstate the stillness of the gaze. A white horse and puffs of smoke were what he remembered from a pulsating celebration of the life and glorious death of the German nationalist hero Theodor Körner. Similarly, his account of *Slaves of Gold*, a Gaumont Western featuring a millionaire on a mission, remains oblivious to plot, but seeks out gesture. 'Mustn't forget him. The calmness, the slow movement, conscious of its goal, a faster step when necessary, a shrug of the shoulder. Rich, spoiled, lulled to sleep, but how he springs up like a servant and searches the room into which he was locked in the forest tavern.'

26 Monday

SUMMER BANK HOLIDAY (NOT SCOT)

27 Tuesday

28 Wednesday

29 Thursday

30 Friday

31 Saturday

1 Sunday

Jonathan Lethem
on Kafka and SF

Is prescience the measure of SF as an art? An attractive tru-
ism says that the best writing about the future is a lens for ap-
prehending the present: Orwell's *Nineteen Eighty-Four* is an X-ray
of 1948, and so forth. Stanisław Lem, in an interview, pointed
out that Kafka's 'In the Penal Colony' isn't better than *The Castle*
for having come true. Then again, perhaps these two things
are really one: to bring oneself to see the present is to see the
future.

Vol. 44 No. 3 · 10 February 2022

2 Monday

3 Tuesday

4 Wednesday

5 Thursday

6 Friday

7 Saturday   8 Sunday

Peter Pulzer
on Kafka and walls

The other wall, the more famous and aesthetically more disting-
uished one, the one designed to protect China from the barbar-
ians, inspired Kafka to one of his most profound reflections:
'Try with all your might to comprehend the decrees of the high
command, but only up to a certain point; then avoid further
meditation.' I do not suppose the rulers of the German Demo-
cratic Republic studied Kafka. They were merely nature imitat-
ing art. For a time they managed to inhibit meditation among
their subjects, though without inducing comprehension. When
meditation resumed, so did comprehension, for reasons Kafka
would have been the first to grasp. The rest we know.

9 Monday

10 Tuesday

11 Wednesday

12 Thursday

13 Friday

The distraction, the weakness of memory, the stupidity! (1915)

14 Saturday　　　　　　　　　　　15 Sunday

Eliot Weinberger
from 'The Wall'

Border guard ███████ was censured for lacking ideological clarity.

Border guard ███████ was censured for sleeping in the watchtower.

Border guard ██████ was censured for telling a comrade that he would like to go the West for just one day to visit a brothel.

Border guard ██████ was censured for lackadaisically performing his early morning gymnastics and not bothering to touch his toes.

Border guard ██████ was censured for copying passages from Franz Kafka in his diary.

Border guard ███████ was censured for owning a toy Mercedes automobile with an integrated measuring tape.

Border guard ██████ was censured for being a committed fan of beat music.

Vol. 34 No. 13 · 5 July 2012

16 Monday

17 Tuesday

18 Wednesday

19 Thursday

Yesterday's letter to Max. Mendacious, vain, theatrical. (1917)

20 Friday

21 Saturday   22 Sunday

Philip Roth
on Kafka and the Prague Spring

Novels *do* influence action, shape opinion, alter conduct – a
book can, of course, change somebody's life – but that's because
of a choice made by the reader to use the fiction for purposes
of his own (purposes that might appal the novelist) and not
because the novel is incomplete without the reader taking action. The 1967 conference near Prague, organised by Czech intellectuals around themes in Kafka, turned out to be a political
stepping-stone to Dubček's reform government and the Prague
Spring of 1968: it was not, however, something that Kafka in-
vited, could have foreseen, or would necessarily have enjoyed.
Ways of knowing the world that he entitled *The Trial* and *The
Castle* – which to most people still look like no way of knowing anything – were exploited by these Czech intellectuals as
a means of organising a perception of *their* world persuasive
enough to augment a political movement already under way to
loosen the bonds of Soviet totalitarianism.

Vol. 9 No. 5 · 5 March 1987

23 Monday

24 Tuesday

My sister said: The apartment (in the story) is very similar to ours. I said: How so? Then the father would have to be living in the water closet. (1912)

25 Wednesday

26 Thursday

27 Friday

28 Saturday   29 Sunday

J.P. Stern
on Kafka and nationalism

Kafka's Prague must be seen as the battleground where various kinds of internecine national strife took place (usually after the pubs were closed), not as a rehearsal of Hitler's 'final solution'. In some ways, Kafka is likely to have experienced this hostility more acutely than did his family and friends: partly because he was more sensitive than they, but partly, too, because the Czechs' hatred was directed above all against the Germans and the 'Germanising' Jews in their midst; and though he did not profess – or indeed feel – any specifically German allegiance, he did after all write in the language of their enemy. He spoke Czech less well than his father (who had come to Prague from a poor Czech-Jewish community in western Bohemia), yet he understood and sympathised with the nascent Czech national-ism. His remarks on 'the literature of small nations', occasion-ed by that visit of the Polish-Jewish actors in 1911, fit the con-temporary state of Czech literature (which he knew well) much better than they do Yiddish literature (in which his interest was slight and intermittent – by 1917 it seems to have been reduced to a small collection of Hassidic stories, 'the only Jewish things . . . I can ever feel at home with, instantly and regardless of what condition I am in'). It is pointless to try to make of him any-thing other than a German writer. A German writer with a differ-ence? Yes, but so were most of his contemporaries in Austria and Germany.

30 Monday

1 Tuesday

2 Wednesday

3 Thursday

4 Friday

5 Saturday   6 Sunday

Marina Warner
on Kafka and Yiddish

'I speak all languages but in Yiddish,' Kafka remarks in his
Diaries; and when it came to writing, he might have chosen any
one of them, besides German. We now read him in all languages,
receiving glimpses, like faraway signals at sea, of the original
German, and beyond the German, of the other languages that
made up Kafka's mindscape, with Yiddish beating out a bass
line, familiar ground.

Vol. 36 No. 8 · 17 April 2014

7　Monday

8　Tuesday

9　Wednesday

10　Thursday

11　Friday

12　Saturday　　　　　　　　　13　Sunday

Dan Jacobson
on Kafka and the Holocaust

Many of Kafka's stories are about people who are tortured and done to death, for reasons which the hypnotised victims can never establish, by an incomprehensibly malign authority. When we read the stories today, it is impossible for us to put out of mind the fate that befell Kafka's sisters, his friends and sweethearts, indeed the entire community of which he was a member. But to speak of his work as if it were directly 'prophetic' of the catastrophe which was to overwhelm the Jews of Central Europe seems to me not only to coarsen the stories but to do much less than justice to the victims of the Nazi massacres. The greatness of Kafka's best tales is that at every moment they open themselves simultaneously to theological, political and psychological interpretation; it denatures the stories to regard any one mode of interpreting them as 'primary', and to imagine that it can be vindicated by historical events of which Kafka himself had no inkling. (That he believed the position of the Jews in Europe to be ultimately hopeless is demonstrated by his support for the Zionist cause: but only hindsight can translate that feeling of hopelessness into a foreknowledge of what was actually to occur.)

14 Monday

An 18-year-old boy comes to say goodbye to us, he is reporting for duty tomorrow: 'Because I am reporting for duty tomorrow, I've come to take my leave of you.' (1917)

15 Tuesday

Leafed through the diary a little. Had a sort of inkling of the organisation of such a life. (1914)

16 Wednesday

17 Thursday

18 Friday

Eternal childhood. Again a call of life. (1921)

19 Saturday   20 Sunday

Michael Wood
on Kafka's aphorisms

Kafka's language is extraordinarily plain and lucid – far more so than that of any other modern writer – but still full of mystery. We can be fairly sure that he is not quite saying what he seems to be saying, but how do we know what else is happening? Kafka is not going to help. His ascetic method is to leave us to it. That is why his novels are themselves full of aphorisms, like these phrases from *The Trial*: 'The text is immutable, and interpreters' opinions are often only an expression of despair over this' and 'Officers of the law don't seek out guilt, but are attracted by guilt.' There is a conflicting, perhaps slightly less hypocritical version of the second claim among the aphorisms themselves: 'A cage went in search of a bird.'

Vol. 44 No. 22 · 17 November 2022

21 Monday

22 Tuesday

Too late. The sweetness of grief and of love. Smiled at her in the boat. That was the most beautiful of all. Always only the longing to die and the still-holding-on, this alone is love. (1913)

23 Wednesday

24 Thursday

25 Friday

26 Saturday   27 Sunday

Judith Butler
on Kafka's parables and Palestine

What does it mean to say 'away-from-here' is 'my destination'? Any place that is not here can be away from here, but any place that becomes a 'here' will not be away from here, but only another here. Is there really any way away from here, or does 'here' follow us wherever we go? What would it mean to be freed of the spatio-temporal conditions of the 'here'? We would not only have to be elsewhere, but that very elsewhere would have to transcend the spatio-temporal conditions of any existing place. So wherever he means to go, it will not be a place as we know a place to be. Is this a theological parable, one that figures an ineffable beyond? Is it a parable about Palestine, the place that in the imagination of the European, according to Kafka, is not a populated place, not a place that can be populated by anyone?

Vol. 33 No. 5 · 3 March 2011

28 Monday

29 Tuesday

30 Wednesday

The firm boundedness of human bodies is ghastly. (1921)

31 Thursday

1 Friday

2 Saturday   3 Sunday

Adam Phillips
on Kafka and tantalisation

In the background of a Kafka story there is often the promise of something, but of something that never happens, as though Kafka's theme is not what was once called existential dread, but tantalisation. The lure of foreclosed possibilities. The very real freedom of being able to turn back, or to give up, seems to be a freedom Kafka fears: he wants to reach the point from which there is no turning back, no turning back from wanting whatever is wanted. And wanted at whatever cost. As though wanting, for Kafka (and not only for Kafka), is like an addiction. The self-cure for having been tantalised is either to turn the tables and become the tantaliser, or to give up on wanting: two forms of revenge, two forms of cruelty to oneself.

Vol. 44 No. 1 · 6 January 2022

4 Monday

5 Tuesday

6 Wednesday

7 Thursday

8 Friday

9 Saturday   10 Sunday

Rivka Galchen
on 'the Brod problem'

I have been, since I can remember, someone not confused by 'the Brod problem': that is, the problem Brod faced of whether or not to follow Kafka's expressed wishes (which seem childish to me) to burn his papers. I just couldn't see the problem. How many elephants can you fit in a Volkswagen? the old joke starts. Three in the back and two in the front. Kafka could have burned the papers himself: the wishes were clearly a cover-up for the real wishes, the true destiny, and who cares about the wishes of the dead anyway? You can perhaps see the excess of practicality and what is sometimes called maturity in play. I felt similarly unmoved by Kafka's famous (boyish) quote about taking an axe to the frozen sea within us. Sure, yes, but also ice-skating; let's be reasonable.

Vol. 39 No. 6 · 16 March 2017

11 Monday

12 Tuesday

13 Wednesday

14 Thursday

15 Friday

I won't let myself get tired. I will jump into my novella even if it should cut up my face. (1910)

16 Saturday   17 Sunday

Patricia Lockwood
on Kafka and copyright

He was coming into the public domain this year; that meant all
of him, she thought. Imagine the feeling of release, being dead
and belonging to the people. Now someone gets to draw a little
cartoon of you, or insert you into their Amish romance; now
you're a character at an off-brand waterpark, trying to cover up
your body as you go mournfully down the slides. Next year, they
will dress freely in his suit in Prague, will extend a hand in him
suddenly, as the rest of the world turns.

Vol. 44 No. 6 · 24 March 2022

18 Monday

19 Tuesday

20 Wednesday

21 Thursday

22 Friday

23 Saturday   24 Sunday

Malin Hay
on BookTok and the canon

The physicality of books is important on BookTok: creators publish 'bookshelf tours' where they explain the arrangement of their shelves (often by colour, but sometimes by genre and trope). Stacks of Penguin Classics go with a specific look: leather jacket, nose piercing, flowers. Works perceived as highbrow are reduced to their covers, or to a combination of fan fiction conventions ('Ms Brontë CREATED every single one of my favourite tropes'). The community is always preparing for battle with the intellectual snob brigade. A recent TikTok by a moody-looking teenager calling herself @ratparade with the text 'you are on the colleen hoover side of booktok I am on the dostoevsky and kafka side we are not the same' prompted a barrage of responses calling the canon elitist and anyone who espouses it a status-seeking pick-me.

25 Monday

26 Tuesday

27 Wednesday

28 Thursday

29 Friday

30 Saturday   1 Sunday

Michael Wood
on Kafka on death

In anyone else's work the idea that you die if you do and die if you don't would sound like despair. In Kafka it feels like an invitation, if not exactly to relax, then to accept reality. Or invent something that will feel like acceptance. The language teacher Kafka would say that we can't choose to accept the mess we already have.

Vol. 44 No. 22 · 17 November 2022

2　Monday　　　　　　　　　　ST ANDREW'S DAY SUBSTITUTE DAY (SCOT)

3　Tuesday

4　Wednesday

5　Thursday

How I rage against my mother! I need only to begin speaking with her and I'm annoyed, almost scream. (1913)

6　Friday

7　Saturday　　　　　　　　　8　Sunday

Will Self
on Kafka's diagnosis

The lesions Kafka was suffering in August 1917, he wrote in a letter to Max Brod, were a 'symbol' of the greater 'wound' – a manifestation of a deep-seated malaise. The proleptic quality of the wound examined by the country doctor closes the first of the rings that ripple out from the fact of Kafka's tuberculosis, through his writings and into the wider world. Rings of co-incidence – or situational irony, since the impact that caused them occurred years before, as is attested by their precursors in Kafka's writings *before* his diagnosis. That Kafka should suffer and die from tuberculosis would be ironic were it not that so many others did as well. Kafka initially saw his illness not as a tragedy but as a 'Blighty wound', allowing for his speedy return home from the frontline of workaday toil and suffering to a *Heimat* of pacific preoccupation. That Kafka's death in 1924 comes at a sort of fulcrum point in time between the dissections of the Parisian doctors René Laënnec, Gaspard Bayle and Pierre Louis – whose combined efforts established both a prospective aetiology and epidemiology for the disease – and the discovery of streptomycin as an effective therapeutic drug in the 1940s, would seem to be just another of those ironic rings.

From 'Kafka's Wound', a digital essay created by the LRB for the Space in 2012.

9 Monday

10 Tuesday

11 Wednesday

12 Thursday

13 Friday

14 Saturday   15 Sunday

Alan Bennett
on the night before Kafka died

In the last weeks of his life Kafka was taken to a sanatorium in the Wienerwald and here, where the secret of dreams had been revealed to Freud, Kafka's dreams ended.

On the windowsill the night before he died, Dora Dymant found an owl waiting. The owl has a complex imagery in art. Just as in Freudian psychology an emotion can stand for itself and for its opposite, so is the owl a symbol of both darkness and light. As a creature of the night, the owl was seen as a symbol of the Jews, who, turning away from the light of Christ, were guilty of wilful blindness. On the other hand, the owl was, as it remains, a symbol of wisdom. It is fitting that this bird of ambiguity should come to witness the departure of a man who by belief was neither Christian nor Jew and had never whole-heartedly felt himself a member of the human race. He had written of himself as a bug and a mouse – both of them the natural prey of the bird now waiting outside the window.

Vol. 9 No. 14 · 23 July 1987

16 Monday

'The thunderous cry of delight from the seraphim.' (1913)

17 Tuesday

Zeno answered an urgent question as to whether nothing ever rests: Yes the flying arrow rests. (1910)

18 Wednesday

19 Thursday

20 Friday

21 Saturday   22 Sunday

Jenny Diski
on writers, sitting alone

And those writers, what are they up to, also sitting alone, making or remaking worlds that are not present, for unknown readers to step into? Solitary writers, solitary readers, unsocialised, silent, engaging with each other by means of the page. It is, when you come to think of it, a bit creepy – a relationship of intense absence. The external observer's fear is of a spiralling down into obsession and madness on the part of the reader who lives only between the covers of a book, or the writer whose entire existence takes place between her sentences. Kafka disappeared into the very letters of his words: 'I can't understand it and I can't believe it. I live only here and there in a small word ("thrust" for instance) in whose vowel I lose my useless head for a moment. The first and last letters are the beginning and end of my fishlike emotion.'

23 Monday

24 Tuesday

25 Wednesday CHRISTMAS DAY

26 Thursday BOXING DAY

27 Friday

28 Saturday 29 Sunday

Franz Kafka
translated by Michael Hofmann
from 'Unknown Laws'

One day a time will come when tradition and its study will reach full term, everything will have been made clear, the law will have become the property of the people, and the nobility will have disappeared. This is not said with any animus towards the nobility, not at all and not by anyone; better to hate ourselves because we are not yet able to be found worthy of the law. And that is why this on the face of it very attractive opinion, which believes in no law as such, has remained so small, because it completely accepts the nobility and its right to exist. There is a necessary self-contradiction here: a party that would reject the nobility as well as belief in the laws would straightaway have the entire population behind it, but such a party cannot come into being, because no one dares to reject the nobility. We live on the razor's edge. An author once put it this way: the only visible un-questionable law that has been imposed on us is the nobility, and who are we to rob ourselves of the only law we have?

Vol. 37 No. 14 · 16 July 2015

30 Monday

31 Tuesday

1 Wednesday   NEW YEAR'S DAY

2 Thursday   2ND JANUARY (SCOT)

3 Friday

4 Saturday   5 Sunday

NOTES

About the LRB

The *London Review of Books* is Europe's leading magazine of culture and ideas. Published twice a month, it provides a space for many of the world's best writers to explore a wide variety of subjects in exhilarating detail – from art and politics to science and technology via history and philosophy, fiction and poetry. In the age of the long read, the LRB remains the pre-eminent exponent of the intellectual essay, admired around the world for its fearlessness, its range and its elegance.

As well as book reviews and reportage, each issue also contains poems, reviews of exhibitions and movies, 'short cuts', letters and a diary, and is available in print, online, and offline via our app. Subscribers enjoy unlimited access to every piece published since 1979, the year the magazine was founded, on our website (our online archive contains all the entries in this volume, and many more that might have made the cut). On lrb.co.uk you'll also find a regular blog, our latest podcasts (including mini-series, Close Readings courses and recordings of events) and occasional films, plus news and recommendations from the London Review Bookshop and Cake Shop. All the volumes on the facing page, as well as other LRB merchandise, are available from our online store.

A reader recently described the LRB as 'the best thing about being a human'. Make it the highlight of your fortnight, too, by subscribing: lrb.me/sub